World Book's Human Body Works

The Circulatory System

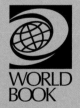

WORLD
BOOK

a Scott Fetzer company
Chicago

www.worldbookonline.com

World Book, Inc.
233 N. Michigan Ave.
Chicago, IL 60601 U.S.A.

For information about other World Book publications, visit our Web site at **http://www.worldbook.com** or call **1-800-WORLDBK (967-5325)**. For information about sales to schools and libraries, call **1-800-975-3250 (United States); 1-800-837-5365 (Canada).**

World Book, Inc.
Editor in Chief: Paul A. Kobasa
Managing Editor: Maureen Mostyn Liebenson
Graphics and Design Manager: Sandra M. Dyrlund
Research Services Manager: Loranne K. Shields
Permissions Editor: Janet T. Peterson

Product development: Arcturus Publishing Limited
Writer: Chris Oxlade
Editor: Alex Woolf
Designer: Jane Hawkins

Library of Congress Cataloging-in-Publication Data
The circulatory system.
     p. cm. -- (World book's human body works)
   Summary: "An introduction to the circulatory system of the human   body--one of six volumes in a set titled WORLD BOOK'S HUMAN BODY WORKS. Includes illustrations, glossary, resource list, and index"--Provided by publisher.
   Includes bibliographical references and index.
   ISBN-13: 978-0-7166-4427-9
   ISBN-10: 0-7166-4427-4
   1. Cardiovascular system--Juvenile literature. 2. Heart--Juvenile literature. I. World Book, Inc. II. Series.
QP103.C57 2007
612.1--dc22
                     2006014110

World Book's Human Body Works (set)
ISBN 13: 978-0-7166-4425-5
ISBN 10: 0-7166-4425-8

Printed in China

07 08 09 10 5 4 3

Acknowledgments
Corbis: cover and 45 (Pete Saloutos), 5 (Tom and Dee Ann McCarthy), 15 (Tom Stewart).
Michael Courtney: 4, 12, 28, 32, 38.
Miles Kelly Art Library: 17.
Science Photo Library: 6 (BSIP Estiot), 7 (Carlyn Iverson), 8 (BSIP/VEM), 9, 10 (Dr. P Marazzi), 11 (Du Cane Medical Imaging Ltd), 13 (SIU), 14 (CNRI), 16 (Lauren Shear), 18 (Paul Rapson), 19 (AJ Photo), 20 (Susumu Nishinaga), 21 (Chemical Design), 22 (Stem Jems), 23, 24 (NIBSC), 25 (Steve Gschmeissner), 26 (BSIP, Lenee), 27 (Mauro Fermariello), 29 (BSIP, Beranger), 30 (Saturn Stills), 31 (David Mack), 33 (Faye Norman), 34 (Biophoto Associates), 35 (Steve Gschmeissner), 36 (Steve Gschmeissner), 37 (Ian Hooton), 39 (Saturn Stills), 40 (BSIP VEM), 41 (Dr. Gopal Murti), 42 (Stevie Grand), 43 (Science Source), 44 (Martin Bond).

Note: The content of this book does not constitute medical advice. Consult appropriate health-care professionals in matters of personal health, medical care, and fitness.

Features included in this book:

- **FAQs** Each spread contains an FAQ panel. FAQ stands for Frequently Asked Question. The panels contain answers to typical questions that relate to the topic of the spread.

- **Glossary** There is a glossary of terms on pages 46–47. Terms defined in the glossary are *italicized* on their first appearance on any spread.

- **Additional resources** Books for further reading and recommended Web sites are listed on page 47. Because of the nature of the Internet, some Web site addresses may have changed since publication. The publisher has no responsibility for any such changes nor for the content of cited resources.

Contents

What is blood circulation?

The human body is a complex machine. It is made up of billions and billions of tiny *cells*. Each cell has a job to do. For example, some cells carry *nerve* signals, some cells make up the skin, and other cells that make up *muscle* enable movements. The main job of blood circulation is to keep all of the cells supplied with the substances they need to do their work. The circulatory system is the network of organs and vessels (tubes) through which blood travels in the body. You can think of blood cells as trucks carrying supplies, and blood vessels as the roads blood cells follow.

Jobs of blood

Blood does the following important jobs for us:

- It carries oxygen from the *lungs* to the cells.

- It carries *nutrients* to the cells.

- It carries wastes away from the cells.

- It protects against disease.

- It helps to repair damage to the blood vessels.

- It carries chemical "messengers" called *hormones* throughout the body.

- It spreads heat throughout the body.

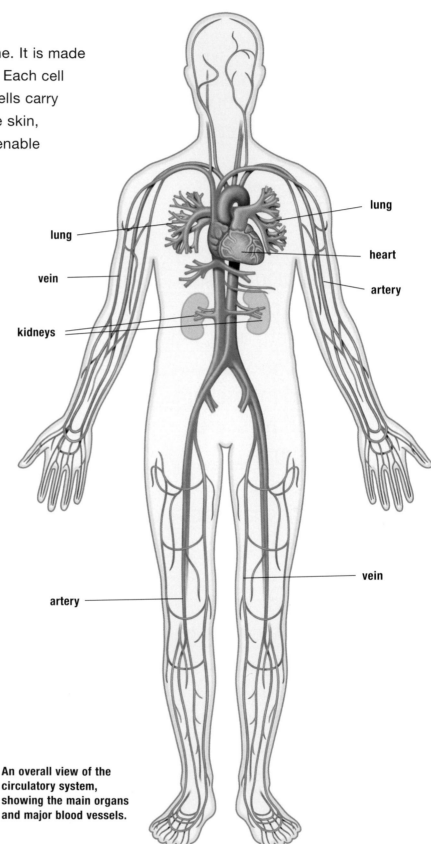

An overall view of the circulatory system, showing the main organs and major blood vessels.

lung

lung

heart

vein

artery

kidneys

vein

artery

Parts of the circulatory system

The circulatory system is made up of the blood; the blood vessels, through which blood travels throughout the body; and the heart, which pumps blood through the blood vessels. The circulatory system has three types of blood vessel: *arteries*, *capillaries*, and *veins*. Arteries carry blood away from the heart to almost all parts of the body. Arteries divide, becoming narrower and narrower until they turn into the narrowest blood vessels, the capillaries. The capillaries take the blood to the body's cells before it flows into the veins for its return journey to the heart. The heart pumps blood using muscles that contract (squeeze) and relax.

Circulatory system care

If the blood vessels become blocked, or the heart stops pumping, blood circulation stops and cells begin to die. So it is vitally important for us to keep our heart and blood vessels healthy.

FAQ

Q. Who discovered blood circulation?

A. English physician William Harvey (1578–1657) discovered how blood circulates in human beings and other mammals. He described the heart as a pump and the circulation of the blood throughout the body in a closed system.

The blood carries energy-giving chemicals to the muscles when we exercise.

The heart

The heart is the most important single part of the circulatory system. The human heart is at the front of the chest, just behind the ribs and slightly to the left of center. The heart is a little larger than the size of its owner's clenched fist. The heart weighs between 9 and 11 ounces (252–308 grams).

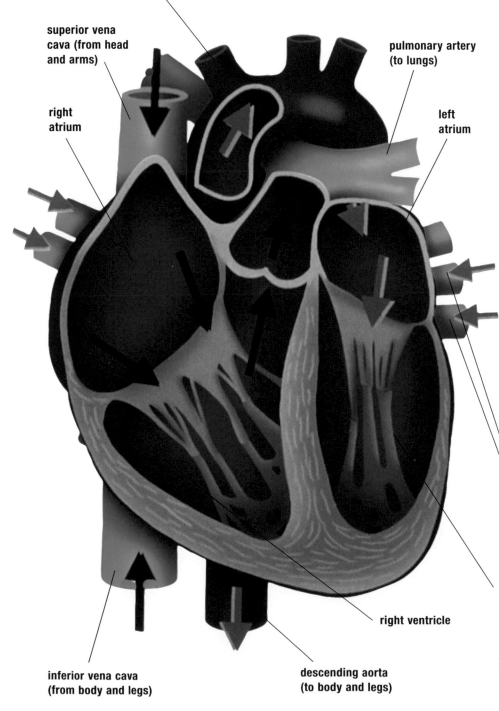

ascending aorta
(to head and arms)

superior vena
cava (from head
and arms)

right
atrium

pulmonary artery
(to lungs)

left
atrium

pulmonary veins
(from lungs)

left ventricle

right ventricle

inferior vena cava
(from body and legs)

descending aorta
(to body and legs)

Heart chambers

Inside the heart are four hollow spaces called chambers. Two are on the right side, and two are on the left side. On each side, the chamber at the top is called the atrium, and the larger chamber at the bottom is called the ventricle. Blood moves into and out of the heart's four chambers through large blood vessels. Blood from the *lungs* goes into the left side of the heart, and the heart pumps it to the rest of the body. Blood from the body goes into the right side of the heart, and the heart pumps it to the lungs.

A cutaway view of the heart showing the internal chambers and main blood vessels.

Heart valves

On each side of the heart, blood flows from an atrium to a ventricle. Between each atrium and ventricle is a one-way *valve* that keeps blood from flowing back again. Each ventricle also has a one-way valve to keep blood from flowing back into the ventricle after it has been pumped out into the *arteries*.

The heart's wall

The heart is made mostly of heart *muscle*, also called cardiac muscle or myocardium. The thin *tissue* lining the heart's chambers is called the endocardium. The thin tissue covering the outside of the heart is called the epicardium. The whole heart is enclosed in a bag-shaped tissue called the pericardium. The muscles on the left side of the heart are the strongest, because they have to push blood all over the body, not only to the lungs. The heart muscle needs its own supply of blood to work. This blood is delivered to the heart through the *coronary arteries*.

An external view of the human heart.

superior vena cava

ascending aorta

pulmonary arteries

coronary arteries

venae cavae

heart muscle

FAQ

Q. When does the heart start working?

A. The heart is one of the first parts of the body to start working before birth. The heart begins to beat eight months before a child is born. In a lifetime of 80 years, the heart will beat about 3 billion times. Unlike the other muscles in the body, healthy heart muscle never gets tired.

Pumping blood

The heart is like two pumps side by side. Each pump pushes blood through a separate closed loop of blood vessels. Blood travels to and from the *lungs* through one of the loops. Blood travels to and from the rest of the body through the other loop. This system is called double circulation.

Double circulation is important for respiration. Respiration is the process by which human beings and other living things get and use oxygen and get rid of the waste made when oxygen is used. In one loop the blood goes to the lungs to collect oxygen. In the other loop blood gives up oxygen to the *cells*. The blood carries waste in the form of the *gas* carbon dioxide in the other direction, from the cells to the lungs.

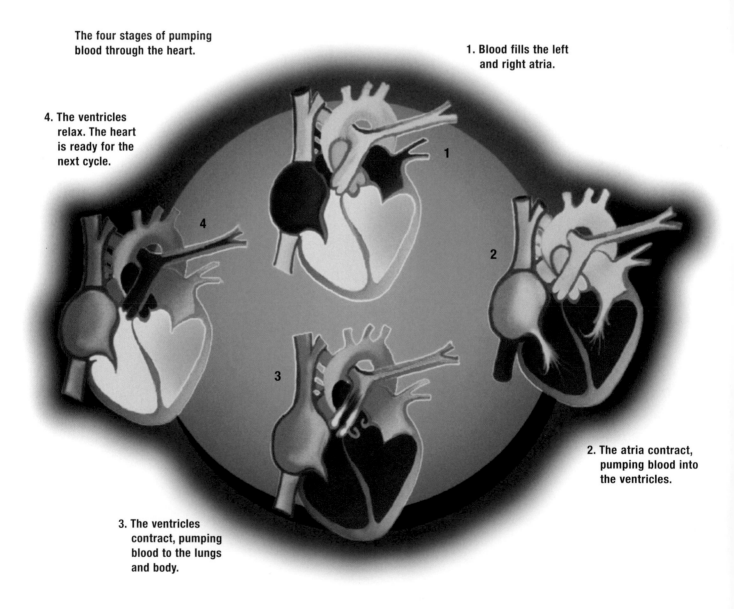

The four stages of pumping blood through the heart.

1. Blood fills the left and right atria.

4. The ventricles relax. The heart is ready for the next cycle.

2. The atria contract, pumping blood into the ventricles.

3. The ventricles contract, pumping blood to the lungs and body.

The pumping action is powered by the heart *muscle*. This muscle keeps contracting and relaxing. During contractions, the heart's chambers get smaller, forcing the blood out and into the blood vessels.

Pumping stages

The heart pumps blood in two stages. When the muscles of the atria are relaxed, blood flows into the heart from the *veins*. It fills the left atrium and the right atrium. Then the muscles of the atria contract, making the two chambers smaller. The pressure of the blood pushes open the one-way *valves* between the atria and their ventricles, and blood flows into the ventricles. This stage of the pumping process is called diastole.

In the next stage, called systole, the stronger muscles around the ventricles contract. This forces blood into the pulmonary *artery* (the blood vessel leading to the lungs) and the *aorta* (the blood vessel leading to the rest of the body). The pressure of the blood closes the flaps of the valves to the atria, keeping blood from flowing back into them. While this is happening, the muscles of the atria relax and the atria refill with blood. Blood tries to flow back into the heart from the pulmonary artery and aorta, but the valves at the top of the ventricles close to block it.

Now the cycle repeats. When a person is resting, the cycle takes just under a second. *Nerves* in the heart itself automatically control the muscle contractions (see page 10).

FAQ

Q. How much blood can the heart pump?

A. When a person is resting, his or her heart pumps about 2.5 fluid ounces (75 cubic centimeters) of blood in each pumping cycle. It pumps an amount equal to slightly more than the blood in an adult's body—about 5 1/4 quarts (5 liters)—about once a minute. In a lifetime of 80 years, the heart pumps about 55 million gallons (208 million liters) of blood. That is enough to fill 83 Olympic-size swimming pools!

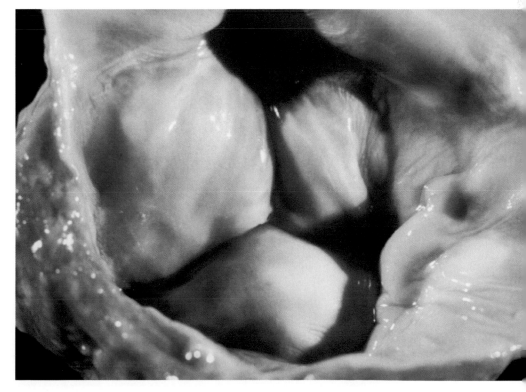

This is a pulmonary valve that prevents blood from the pulmonary arteries from flowing back into the right ventricle.

The heartbeat

Each two-stage contraction of the cardiac *muscles* that causes blood to flow into the *arteries* is called a heartbeat. Our nervous system automatically controls the timing of each heartbeat and the heart rate (the number of beats per minute). We also think of the heartbeat as the sound a heart makes. Each beat creates a "lub-dub" sound, which a person can hear through a device called a *stethoscope*. The sound is not made by the heart muscles contracting, but by the *valves* in the heart snapping shut under pressure.

Triggering the beat

Each beat of the heart is triggered by *nerve* signals, which are electric currents that travel along nerve *cells*. The signals start in a tiny group of cells called the sinoatrial node, or pacemaker. About every second, the heart pacemaker makes a signal. The signal spreads through the muscles in the atria, making them contract and force blood into the ventricles. Another group of cells detects the signals and passes them along a special nerve pathway to the bottom of the ventricles. Then the signals enter the muscles around the ventricles. The muscle contractions start at the bottom of the ventricles and move up. This forces the blood up and out of the ventricles.

An electrocardiogram shows the electrical signals in the heart as it beats.

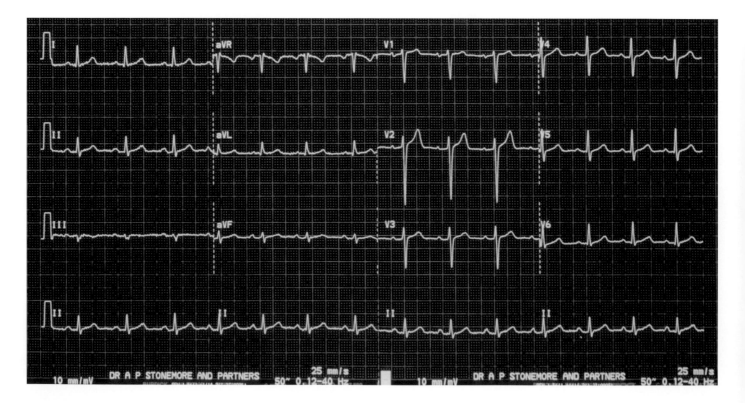

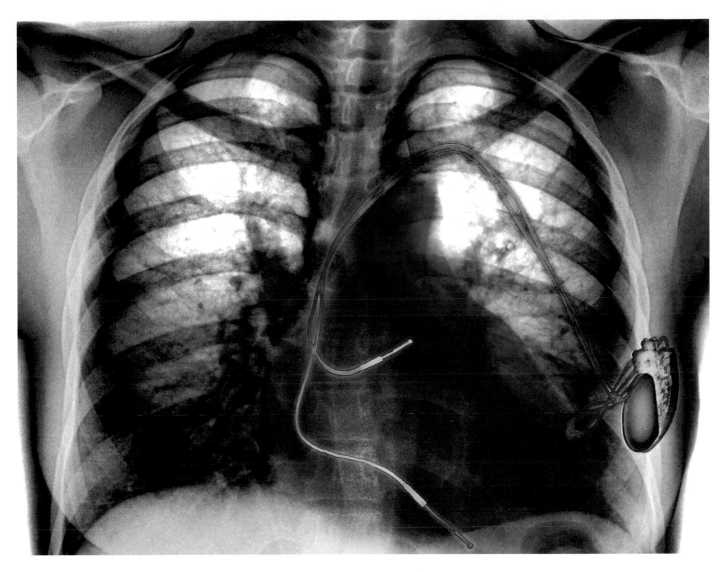

This X-ray shows an artificial pacemaker (bottom right) and its electrodes connected to the heart.

Changing the rate

During vigorous activity, our muscles need more oxygen and *glucose* (a kind of sugar), which is fuel for the muscle cells. The muscles therefore need more blood, and so the heart starts pumping faster to supply it. After the activity stops, the heart slows down again. Our brain automatically controls the changes of heart rate.

FAQ

Q. What is an artificial pacemaker?

A. A normal heart beats very regularly, with the same delay between each beat. But sometimes the beat becomes irregular, and the heart stops working efficiently. For some people, an artificial, electronic pacemaker solves this problem. An artificial pacemaker is a small, battery-operated device that is implanted in a person's chest. If the person's heart beats irregularly, the pacemaker sends an electric signal through wires to the heart. The signal makes the cardiac muscle contract at a proper rate and rhythm.

Arteries

Arteries are the vessels through which blood travels away from the heart. The heart pumps blood into two arteries: the pulmonary artery and the *aorta*. The pulmonary artery divides into two arteries, one for each lung. The aorta goes down through the abdomen. Arteries branch off from the aorta to the head, the arms, and the organs, such as the liver and the kidneys. The arteries also divide to carry blood to the *intestines* and down each leg. The large arteries have names (see table).

Some major arteries

aorta	to the body
pulmonary arteries	to the lungs
carotid arteries	to the head and neck
coronary arteries	to the heart
subclavian arteries	to the arms
femoral arteries	to the legs
hepatic artery	to the liver
iliac arteries	to the abdomen

The arteries continue dividing and getting narrower, like the branches of a tree. Millions of tiny arteries carry blood to nearly all parts of the body. The smallest arteries are called arterioles.

The internal structure of an artery.

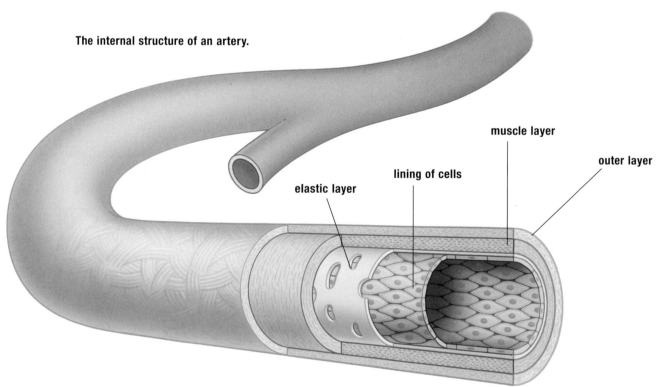

muscle layer

outer layer

lining of cells

elastic layer

Artery structure

The heart pumps blood into the arteries in strong surges. The arteries are the strongest of the blood vessels, which allows them to withstand the pressure of these surges.

Artery walls have three layers. The inner layer keeps blood from leaking out and is smooth to allow blood to flow easily. The middle layer is made of *muscle*, which allows the artery to stretch and then return to its original shape. The outer layer is made of tough, stretchy tissue.

As a surge of blood comes from the heart, the artery stretches to let it through. Then the artery returns to its original shape, squeezing the blood and giving it an extra push along the artery. The muscles in the artery walls can change the width of an artery and so control the amount of blood that flows through the artery.

FAQ

Q. How wide are arteries?

A. The widest artery is the aorta. The space inside the aorta is about an inch (25 millimeters) across. A medium-sized artery is about 0.2 inch (5 millimeters) across. Arterioles are about the width of a human hair.

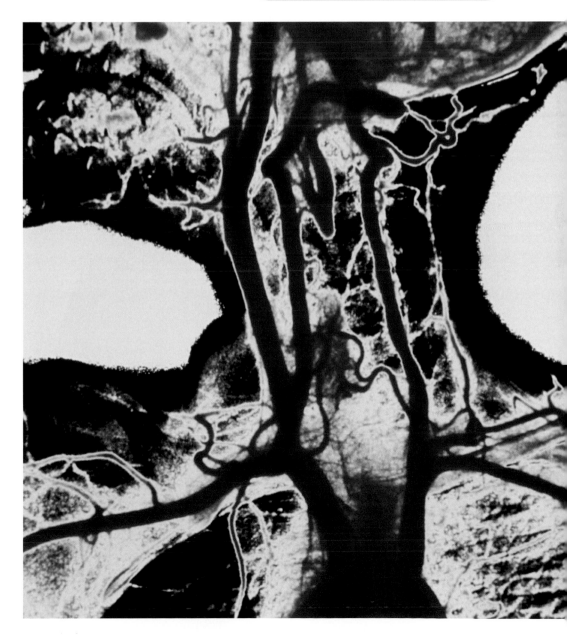

In this special X-ray, called an angiogram, a dye has been injected into arteries to make them more visible. These are carotid arteries.

Capillaries

The *arteries* deliver blood from the heart throughout the body. When the blood reaches the tissues of the organs and other parts of the body, it flows into different types of blood vessels, called *capillaries*. As the blood flows through the capillaries, oxygen, *nutrients*, and other substances move from the blood into *cells*. Waste chemicals from the cells move the other way, from the cells into the blood.

You have millions of capillaries in your body. Most of them are less than 0.04 inch (1 millimeter) long, but all the capillaries lined up end to end would stretch 50,000 miles (80,500 kilometers). Nearly every cell in your body is close to a capillary.

A pink face is a sign that more blood than usual is flowing through the capillaries in the skin.

FAQ

Q. Why do I turn red when I run around?

A. One of the jobs of the circulatory system is to disperse (spread) heat evenly around the body. When you run, the cells in your *muscles* produce heat that needs to be released so your body does not overheat. The blood carries excess heat to your skin. There the heat can escape into the air. If you are light skinned, the blood flowing to your skin makes it red. As you cool down, blood flow to the skin surface returns to normal and the red "flush" fades.

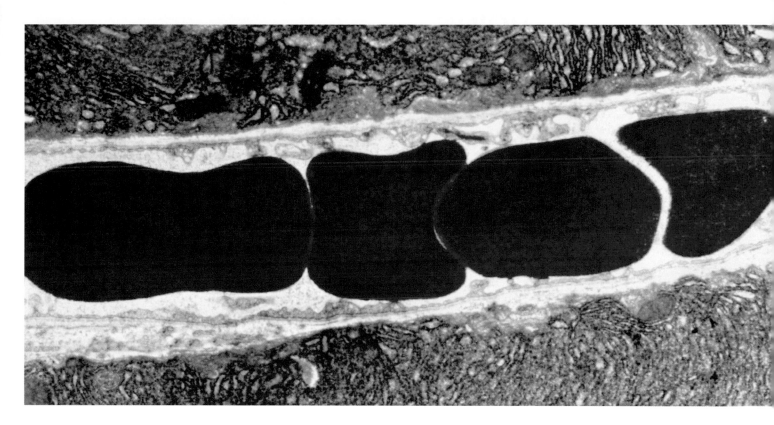

Capillary networks

The *tissues* that make up the parts of the body are riddled with capillaries. The capillaries divide, spreading through the tissues and supplying blood to all the cells there. Beyond where they spread into the tissues, the capillaries join up again, making larger and larger blood vessels until they link up with the *veins*. The veins are the vessels through which the blood travels back to the heart. The branches of capillaries that divide and join up again are called capillary networks. Many capillaries are so narrow that blood cells can squeeze through them only in single file.

A magnified image showing red blood cells passing through a capillary.

Capillary structure

The walls of a capillary are only one cell thick. They do not have layers like those of artery walls. Capillary walls are so thin that most of the ingredients that make up blood can pass through them to reach the cells outside the walls. This allows nutrients, oxygen, and wastes to be exchanged (traded) between the blood cells and the tissue cells. Red blood cells cannot pass through capillary walls.

Veins

Veins are the vessels through which blood travels from the *lungs* and the rest of the body back to the heart. Blood from the many millions of *capillaries* in your body flows into the veins. About two thirds of the body's blood is in the veins at any time. The large veins leading from the internal organs and large sections of the body have names (see table on page 17).

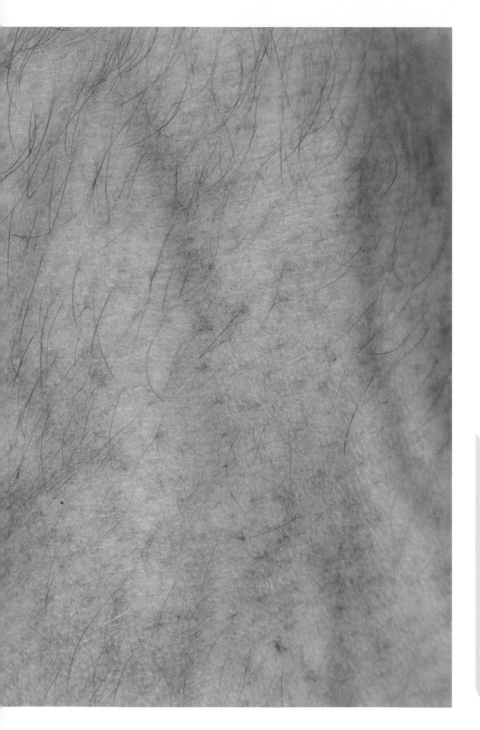

A close-up of human skin. The blue lines are veins beneath the skin.

Joining veins

Blood from capillaries flows into tiny veins, called venules, which are microscopically small. Venules gradually join with each other, making wider veins that carry more and more blood. They are like small streams running through a valley, joining to make larger streams and then rivers. Eventually all the blood from the body flows into two large veins that lead to the heart. These veins are the inferior

FAQ

Q. How can blood flow uphill?

A. Blood flows up to your head from your heart because your heart pumps the blood up there. But how does blood get from your feet back to your heart? The answer is that large veins run through the *muscles* that make your legs move. When these muscles contract, blood is pushed up through the veins. The valves in the veins make sure that the blood flows only up toward the heart.

vena cava, which brings blood from the lower part of body, and the superior vena cava, which brings blood from the upper part of the body. The two pulmonary veins bring blood back to the heart from the two lungs.

Some major veins

superior vena cava	from the upper body
inferior vena cava	from the lower body
pulmonary veins	from the lungs
jugular veins	from the head
brachial veins	from the arms
femoral veins	from the legs
hepatic veins	from the liver, pancreas, stomach, gallbladder
portal vein	from the intestines to the liver

Vein structure

The walls of veins have three layers, just like *artery* walls. However, because blood does not surge through the veins as it does through the arteries, veins are not as tough as arteries and have thinner walls. Every few inches along most of the larger veins is a one-way *valve* that keeps blood from flowing backward, away from the heart.

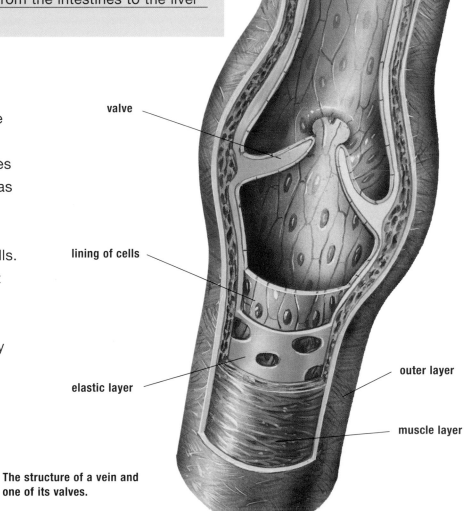

valve

lining of cells

elastic layer

outer layer

muscle layer

The structure of a vein and one of its valves.

Parts of the blood

As you have learned, blood is the thick liquid that flows in the circulatory system. Pumped by the heart through the vessels, the blood transports the substances that the body needs or must get rid of.

Blood is a complex mixture of different ingredients. Each ingredient has a job to do. As the blood flows through the *capillaries*, substances move back and forth between the blood and the surrounding *cells*. Blood is made up of a liquid called *plasma*, with substances dissolved in it, together with cells known as *formed elements*. An adult who weighs 160 pounds (73 kilograms) has about 5 quarts (4.7 liters) of blood. This amounts to about 8 percent of an adult's body weight.

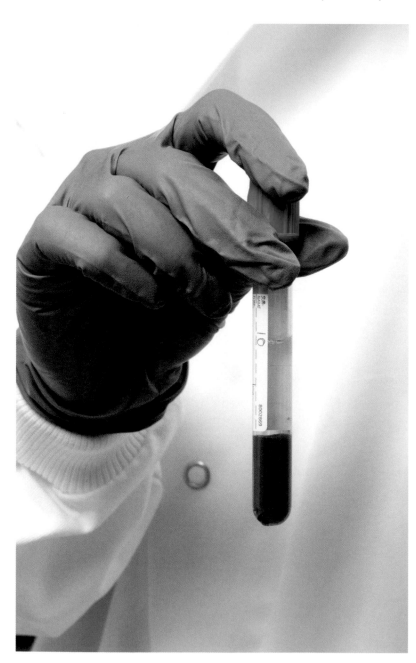

This blood sample has been spun in a centrifuge to separate it into plasma (top) and formed elements (bottom).

Blood plasma

If a sample of blood is left in a clear tube, you could see the formed elements slowly settle to the bottom, leaving a yellowish liquid above. This liquid is plasma. It is more than 90 percent water, and the rest is made up of substances dissolved in the water.

Some of these substances are transported around the body. They include *minerals*, such as sodium and potassium; waste from the cells, such as the *gas* carbon dioxide; *glucose*, which is fuel for the cells; and *hormones*, which are chemical "messengers" that control some of the body's functions. Plasma also contains substances called *proteins*. Proteins are important in building, maintaining, and repairing body *tissues*.

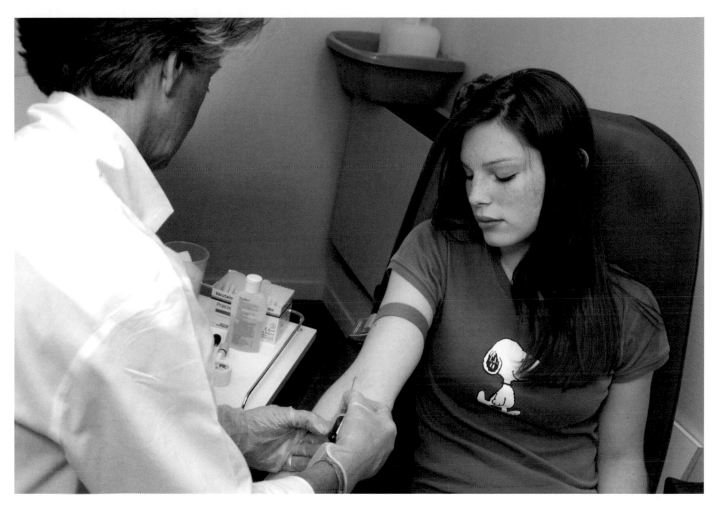

A doctor taking a blood sample. There is a convenient vein on the inside of the elbow.

Specialized proteins called antibodies help shield the body from disease. Other proteins help to clot the blood (see pages 24–25).

Formed elements

There are three formed elements in blood: red blood cells, white blood cells, and *platelets*. Red blood cells (see pages 20–21) transport oxygen; white blood cells (see pages 22–23) fight disease; and platelets (see pages 24–25) stop bleeding at the site of a wound.

FAQ

Q. What is a blood test?

A. A blood test measures the amount of blood cells and other substances in a person's blood and enables doctors to see if the blood appears healthy. If the level of a particular ingredient in a person's blood is higher or lower than normal, or if elements of the blood are larger or smaller than normal or oddly shaped, it could be a sign of a disease or other problem. For example, a high level of the sugar glucose in the blood could show that the person is suffering from diabetes. Diabetes is a disease that reduces the body's ability to use glucose for energy.

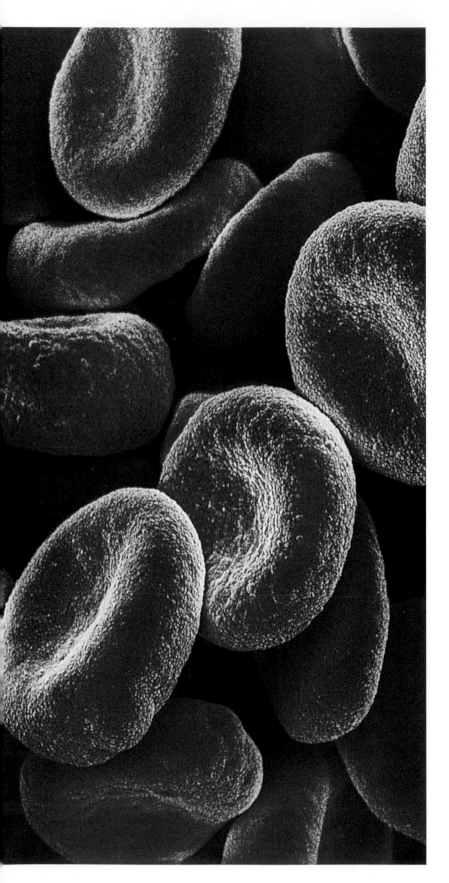

Red blood cells

Red blood *cells*, which are also called erythrocytes, make up nearly half of the volume of a person's blood. The job of red blood cells is to carry oxygen from the *lungs* to all the cells in the body and to carry some of the carbon dioxide from the cells to the lungs. In the cells, oxygen combines with *glucose* in a chemical reaction that releases energy. The cells need energy to do their jobs. The process generates carbon dioxide as a waste product.

Size and shape

Red blood cells are extremely small. Each one is only about 0.0003 inches (0.0075 mm) across, making red blood cells among the smallest cells in the body. A drop of blood the size of a pinhead holds millions of red blood cells. A red blood cell is round and flat with dips in each face, like a doughnut without a hole. Red blood cells easily compress (squash) and stretch to fit through narrow *capillaries*.

Red blood cells are made in the red marrow in the center of bones. Red blood cells live for about 120 days and then die. The marrow is constantly replacing them—at the rate of about 2 million every second!

A micrograph (a photograph taken through a microscope) of red blood cells. This image has been magnified by over 7,000 times.

Collecting and delivering oxygen

Red blood cells collect oxygen in the lungs and release it to cells throughout the body. The oxygen is carried by a special chemical called *hemoglobin*, which attracts oxygen. Every red blood cell contains hundreds of millions of *molecules* of hemoglobin. The molecules are long and folded, and each hemoglobin molecule can carry four molecules of oxygen.

When blood passes through capillaries in the lungs, oxygen from the air we breathe in attaches to the hemoglobin, making oxyhemoglobin. When blood arrives in capillaries all over the body, the oxygen leaves the oxyhemoglobin and moves to the cells.

One of the waste products the cells make is carbon dioxide. Hemoglobin carries some of the carbon dioxide from the cells; but most of it enters the plasma. Both substances carry the carbon dioxide back to the lungs to be breathed out.

FAQ

Q. What makes blood change its color?

A. The oxyhemoglobin in red blood cells when they are carrying oxygen is bright red. This is why blood that comes from the lungs is red. When the red blood cells give up the oxygen to the body's cells, the red blood cells turn a darker, brownish-red color. So blood traveling through the *arteries* from the heart is bright red, and blood traveling through the *veins* toward the heart is brownish-red.

A computer-generated model of a hemoglobin molecule.

White blood cells

White blood *cells*, which are also called leukocytes, are the second main type of blood cell. White blood cells do not transport substances, like *plasma* and red blood cells do. The job of white blood cells is to fight disease (see pages 36–37). The white blood cells work together like an army that attacks invaders in the body, such as *bacteria* and *viruses*.

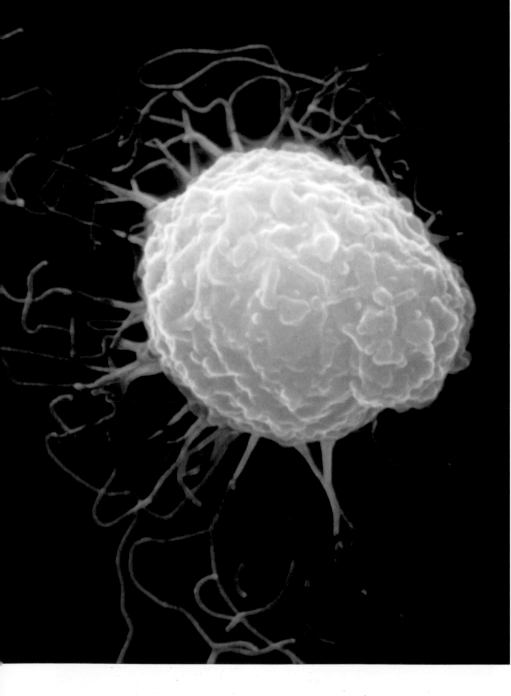

A micrograph of a T-cell lymphocyte.

White blood cells use the circulatory system to move quickly to where they are needed in the body. They move in and out of the blood by squeezing through *capillary* walls. White blood cells are larger than red blood cells, and have a *nucleus*, which red blood cells do not. White blood cells are actually colorless rather than white.

Types of white blood cell

Red blood cells are all the same, but white blood cells come in five main types. Each type of white blood cell has a particular job in fighting disease. The five different types of white blood cell are lymphocytes, basophils, neutrophils, monocytes, and eosinophils. Lymphocytes release chemicals that help fight disease. The two types of lymphocyte are called T cells and B cells. Neutrophils, monocytes, and eosinophils engulf (swallow up) invaders. Monocytes become cells in the body's tissues called macrophages, which digest bacteria. Eosinophils, monocytes, and neutrophils are collectively known as *phagocytes*, which means "cell eaters."

Making white blood cells

All white blood cells start life in bone marrow. They begin as stem cells, which are cells that can turn into any type of cell. Some white blood cells complete their formation in the bone marrow. Others begin forming and then move to other parts of the body to complete their formation. T cells, for example, mature in the thymus *gland*.

The pink objects in the photograph are bacteria. They are being engulfed by a macrophage white blood cell.

FAQ

Q. How many white blood cells do I have?

A. The answer is many billions. Normally the blood has about one white blood cell for at least every 800 red blood cells, but when the body is fighting infection, the number of white blood cells increases. White blood cells live from only a few hours or days to months or years. More are always being produced to replace the dying cells. For example, 100 billion neutrophils are made every day to replace those lost in fighting infections.

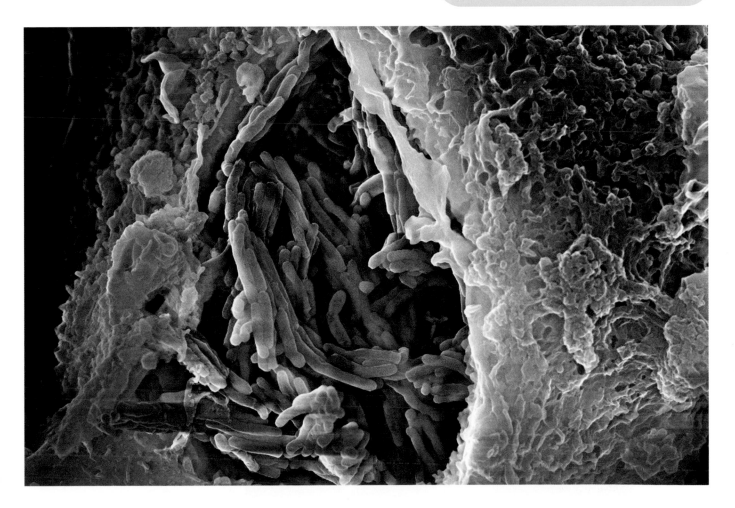

Platelets and clotting

If you accidentally cut your finger or scrape your knee, blood flows out of the wound because blood vessels have been broken. But the flow of blood usually soon stops. The flow stops because the blood itself automatically blocks the breaks in the damaged vessels. This process is called clotting. Clotting keeps more blood from being lost and prevents such foreign objects as *bacteria* from getting into the wound. Clotting is done by *platelets* and *proteins* in the blood.

A micrograph of blood platelets, magnified by 3,300 times.

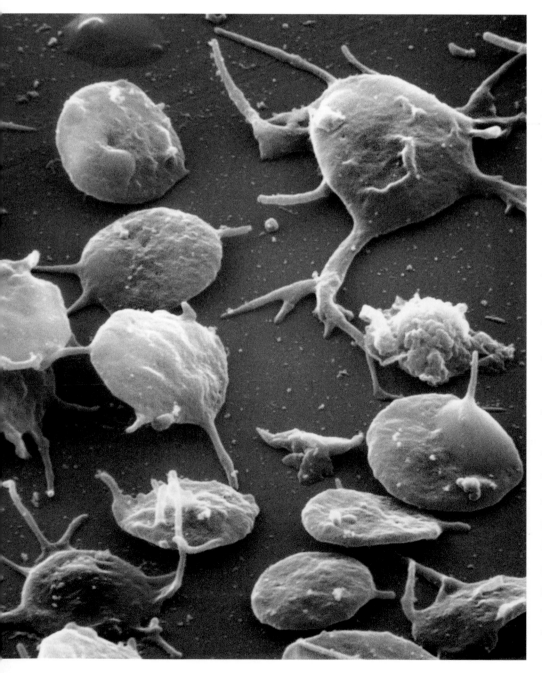

Platelets

Platelets, which are also called thrombocytes, are slightly smaller than red blood cells. A drop of blood the size of a pinhead holds hundreds of thousands of platelets. Platelets are made from giant "parent" cells in the bone marrow. Platelets live for only about 10 days.

The clotting process

When you cut yourself, cells in the walls of blood vessels are damaged. The injured blood vessel quickly contracts to slow the flow of blood through it. Next, platelets cling to the broken cells. They release chemicals into the blood that make more platelets gather at the wound site. The platelets form a plug that helps keep the blood from leaking out.

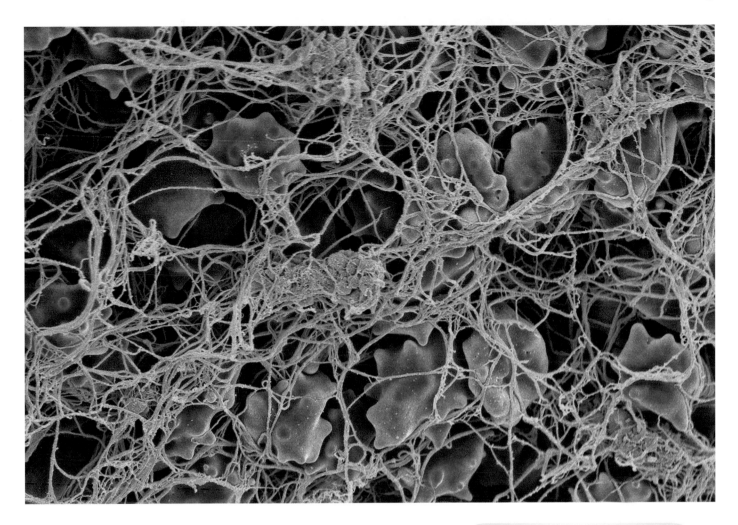

Long threads of fibrin forming a mesh at the site of a wound. The mesh is trapping the red blood cells visible behind it.

Now clotting starts. This is a complex chemical process. There are proteins in *plasma* called clotting factors. These proteins combine with chemicals from the damaged cells and chemicals from platelets. A clotting factor called fibrinogen changes into a solid substance called fibrin. Fibrin forms long threads that knit together to form a mesh over the wound. The mesh traps platelets and blood cells, forming a mass of material. Soon the fibrin threads shorten to squeeze the mass, forming a solid clot that seals the wound. On the skin, the clot appears as a scab. Finally the wound is repaired as new skin forms under the scab.

FAQ

Q. What is hemophilia?

A. Hemophilia is a disease that prevents the blood from clotting normally. A person with hemophilia is known as a hemophiliac. A hemophiliac's blood does not clot properly because one of the clotting factors is missing from his or her blood. Hemophilia is a hereditary disease. A hereditary disease is one coming from the sufferer's parents or ancestors. Women can pass hemophilia to their children, but usually only males suffer from it.

Blood groups

All blood *cells* have *proteins* called antigens on their surface. Each person's red blood cells have a particular antigen or combination of antigens. Blood is classified into groups depending on the antigens present. Blood groups are important in such medical procedures as blood transfusions because mixing two different types of blood in a person can make his or her blood cells clump together. The clumped blood cells clog small blood vessels and keep blood from circulating, which can harm and even kill a person.

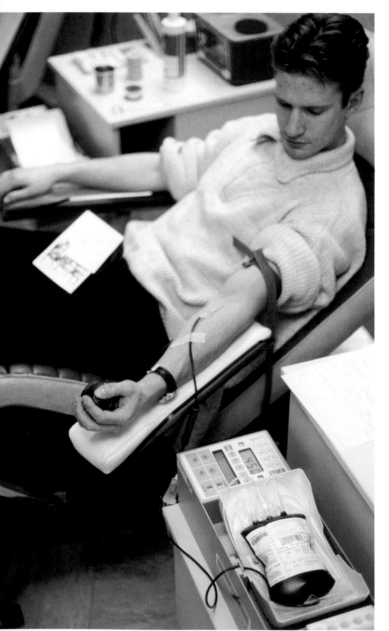

This man is donating blood that will be used for blood transfusions. The bag is carefully labeled with identifying information and blood type.

Antibodies

Antibodies are disease-fighting proteins in the blood (see page 36). Foreign substances in the blood, such as *bacteria*, also have antigens. The antibodies recognize foreign antigens and attack them. A person's own antibodies recognize the antigens on that person's own blood cells and do not attack them. But if blood from two different groups is mixed, the antibodies from one group can attack the blood cells in the other.

FAQ

Q. What is a blood bank?

A. A blood bank is a place where donated blood is stored. A blood bank stores blood of different types in labeled plastic bags, ready to be used. Blood can be stored under refrigeration for up to 42 days, or frozen for several years. Sometimes the cells in the blood are removed to leave the *plasma*. Plasma is given mainly to hemophiliacs, but also to burn victims because burns make plasma leak out of the blood vessels. Plasma can be stored frozen for several years.

ABO blood groups

The most commonly used blood-grouping system is the ABO system. The four main types of blood in this group are A, B, AB, and O. The type of blood depends on whether the blood cells have antigens called A and B. Type A blood has only the A antigen; type B blood has only the B antigen; type AB blood has both the B and the A antigen; and type O blood has neither antigen. Type A blood contains antibodies that attack type B cells, and type B blood contains antibodies that attack type A cells. Type AB blood contains neither antibody, and type O blood contains both.

A person cannot receive blood from a donor whose blood cells would be attacked by antigens in the person's blood. For example, type A blood cannot be given to a person with type B blood. But people with AB blood can receive any type of blood, and type O blood can be given to anybody. For safety, samples of blood from a recipient and a donor are mixed first to make sure no clumping occurs.

Chemical tests are used to establish the blood type of a blood sample.

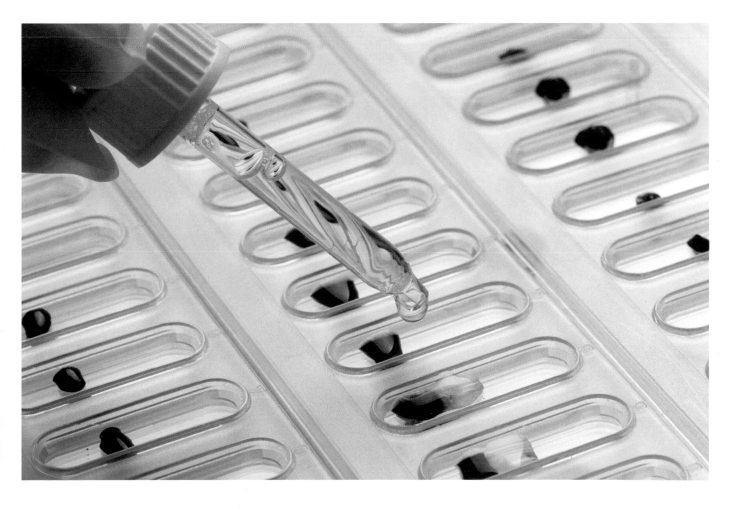

Blood maintenance

Our bodies constantly use and replace the ingredients in blood. The level of different ingredients in the blood must be balanced, and unwanted substances must be removed. These substances include wastes created by the body's own processes and toxins (poisons) that come from outside the body, such as alcohol and pollutants. Worn-out blood *cells* must also be removed. These jobs are carried out mostly by the liver and the spleen (see page 39).

The liver

The liver is a triangular organ, about 8 inches (20 centimeters) long. It is the body's chemical-processing plant. The liver's cells perform hundreds of different tasks. Among them is controlling the level of various *nutrients* in the blood, such as *glucose* and *fats*.

The liver also processes wastes and toxins in the blood. The removal of toxins is called detoxification. The liver breaks toxins down into less harmful chemicals, which go back into the blood.

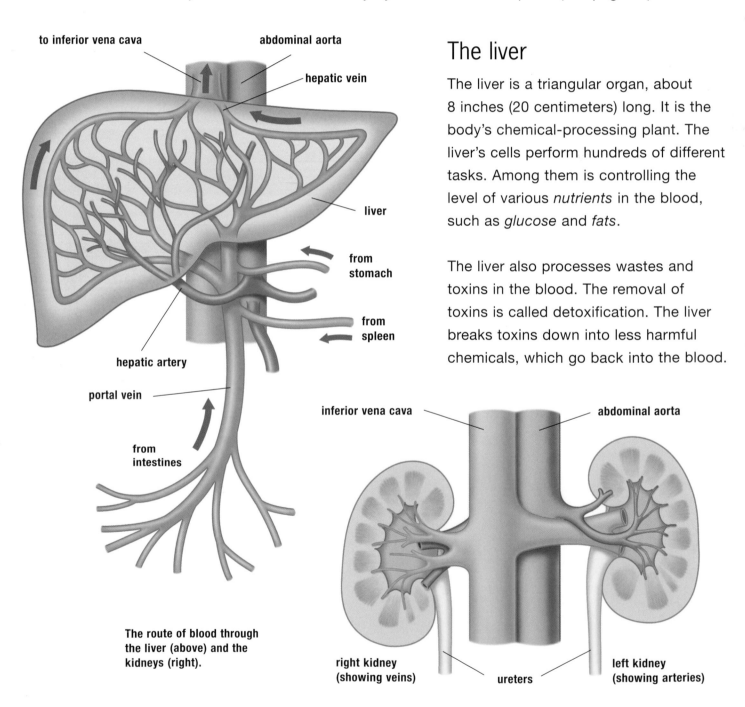

to inferior vena cava

abdominal aorta

hepatic vein

liver

from stomach

from spleen

hepatic artery

portal vein

from intestines

The route of blood through the liver (above) and the kidneys (right).

inferior vena cava

abdominal aorta

right kidney (showing veins)

ureters

left kidney (showing arteries)

For example, ammonia is a toxic waste product from the body's cells. The blood carries it from the cells to the liver. The liver combines it with another waste product, carbon dioxide. This makes a chemical called urea, which then is removed from the blood by the kidneys.

The liver also helps to break down old blood cells. It recovers the iron from the *hemoglobin* and stores it so that it can be used to make new cells.

The kidneys

There are two kidneys, one on each side of the body. Each kidney is about 4.5 inches (11.4 centimeters) long. The kidneys remove waste chemicals and excess water from the blood. Inside each kidney, blood is passed through about a million tiny structures that work as filters. The filters remove almost everything except the blood cells themselves. The filters then return any useful chemicals to the blood. The waste chemicals, such as urea, are passed out of the body in *urine*.

FAQ

Q. Can people get new kidneys and livers?

A. Sometimes the kidneys or liver can stop working properly. A diseased pair of kidneys or liver can be replaced with healthy substitutes in a procedure called a transplant. Usually only one kidney is transplanted because the body really needs only one. Only a small piece of healthy liver needs to be transplanted. Within a few weeks a whole new liver will have grown from it.

A kidney dialysis machine does the job of the kidneys until a patient can receive a transplant.

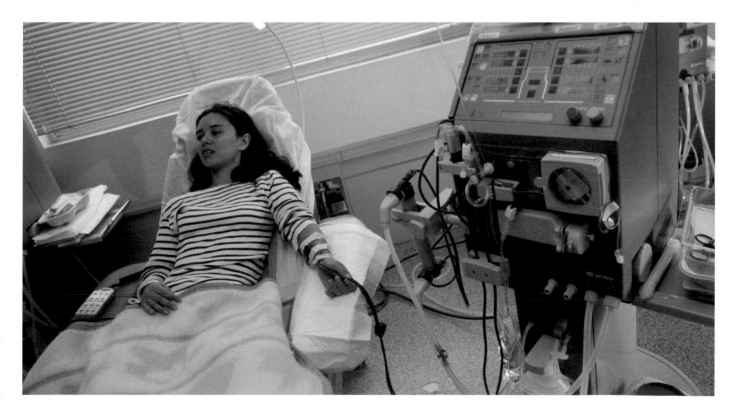

Blood pressure

When you use a bicycle pump to inflate a tire, you can feel the handle of the pump resisting (pushing back) as you push the handle down. This is because pushing down puts the air in the pump under pressure. The heart is a pump, too. When it contracts, it pushes blood into the blood vessels. This puts the blood under pressure and makes it flow through the blood vessels. The pressure of the blood is called blood pressure. Blood pressure makes blood flow out of a wound.

Changing pressure

Blood pressure is highest in the *arteries* close to the heart. It gradually falls as the blood moves farther away from the heart. The pressure in the *capillaries* is quite low, and it is very low in the *veins*. The pressure also rises and falls as the heart beats. It is highest when the ventricles contract, pushing blood into the arteries, and lowest when the cardiac *muscles* relax between beats.

Measuring pressure

Blood pressure is useful for doctors as an indicator of the health of a patient's heart and blood vessels. Because blood pressure is different in different

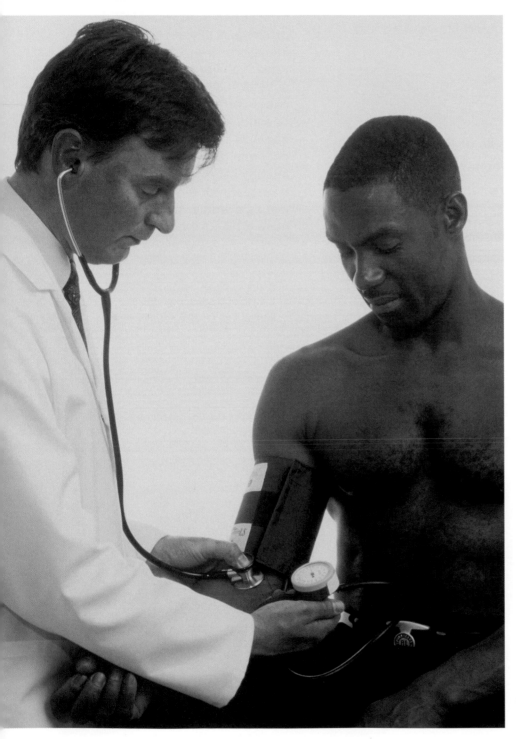

A doctor measuring a patient's blood pressure with a sphygmomanometer.

parts of the body, it is always measured at the same place—the upper arm. This allows doctors to compare blood pressure readings at different times and between different people.

Blood pressure is measured using a device called a sphygmomanometer. Two blood pressure readings are always taken. The first reading is taken when the ventricles are contracting and pressure is at its highest. This is called systolic blood pressure. The second is taken when the heart muscles are relaxed and the pressure is at its lowest. This is called diastolic blood pressure.

The pressure readings are written down together, with the systolic pressure placed over the diastolic pressure. The normal blood pressure for an adult is 120/80, which is read as "120 over 80."

FAQ

Q. What is high blood pressure?

A. When blood pressure is higher than normal—140/90, for example—it is called high blood pressure. High blood pressure is also called hypertension. It can be a sign that blood vessels are slightly blocked or damaged. High blood pressure can damage such organs as the kidneys and eyes and place a strain on the heart. Doctors can help people who have high blood pressure control the condition.

A computer-generated artwork of an artery narrowed by disease. This increases blood pressure in the artery.

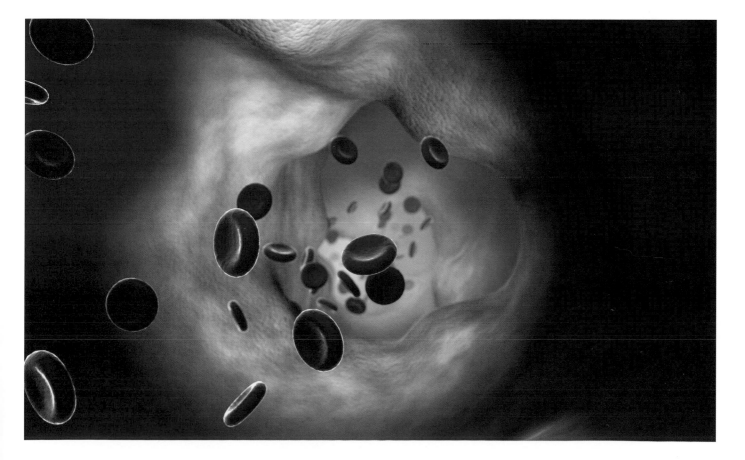

The pulse

Blood does not flow steadily throughout the body. Each beat of the heart sends high-pressure blood surging into the *arteries*. Then, as the heart *muscles* relax, the blood slows down again and the pressure falls. The arteries have stretchy walls that bulge when the rush of blood comes from the heart. The artery walls contract again when the heart relaxes. So at any point on an artery, the artery's walls pulse (move in and out) in time with the heartbeat.

Feeling the pulse

In some places on the body, arteries are close to the surface of the skin and you can feel them pulsating as blood surges through them. In a few places you can even see the skin rise and fall. The best places to feel the pulse are on the sides of the neck, behind the knee, under the arm, and in the wrist. A doctor or nurse finds the pulse by touching one of these places, usually the neck or wrist.

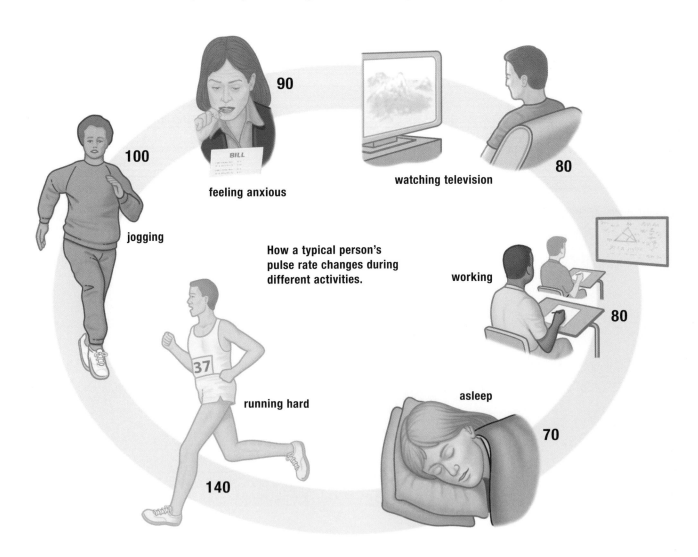

90 feeling anxious

100 jogging

watching television

80

80 working

70 asleep

140 running hard

How a typical person's pulse rate changes during different activities.

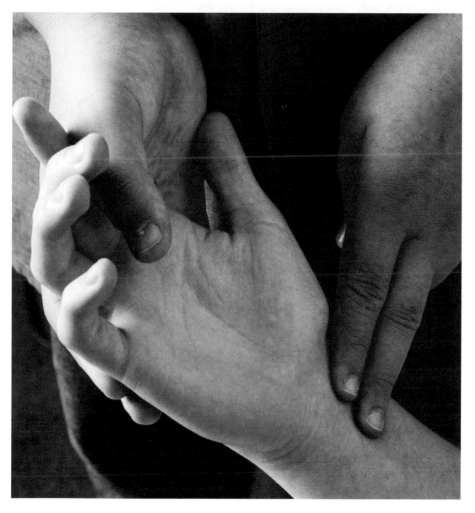

FAQ

Q. Can I measure my own pulse?

A. Here is how you can find and measure your own pulse. Hold your right hand with its palm facing up. Rest the first two fingers of your left hand gently on your right wrist, about an inch (2.5 centimeters) to the right of the middle and an inch (2.5 centimeters) from the base of your hand. You should be able to feel your pulse. Using the second hand of a clock or wristwatch, count the number of pulses in 60 seconds.

A doctor checks a patient's pulse by feeling the inside of her wrist.

Pulse rates

Each pulse represents the completion of one heartbeat. So the pulse tells us how often the heart is beating (the heart rate), although the pulse happens slightly later than the beat. The pulse rate is the number of pulses that happen per minute. The pulse rate of an adult sitting still or sleeping (called the resting pulse rate) is normally between 50 and 100 beats per minute. The rate can more than double during strenuous activity. In young people it can rise to over 200 beats per minute during exercise, for example.

An irregular or fast pulse can be an indication of disease or another problem. So the pulse is one of the first things that doctors check when they are examining a patient. A rate that is faster than average could be a sign of an inefficient heart.

Delivering supplies, collecting trash

The main job of the circulatory system is to take supplies to and wastes from the body's cells. The circulatory system is a transportation system for the *nutrients* and wastes. These substances are carried in the blood, which travels through the blood vessels. Oxygen is carried by the red blood *cells*. Other substances, such as *glucose* and *minerals*, are dissolved in the plasma. The circulatory system carries nutrients to where they are needed. The circulatory system also carries away waste from the cells so that it can be passed out of the body.

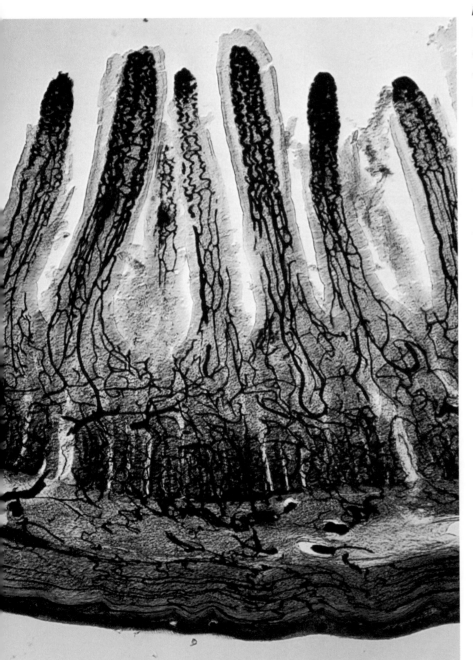

A magnified image of a slice from the wall of the intestine, showing the capillaries that collect nutrients.

Oxygen

Oxygen is vital to keep cells alive. So oxygen is the most important chemical transported by the blood. It is carried by red blood cells. Oxygen passes into the red blood cells in the *lungs* and later passes into the body's cells where they meet *capillaries* throughout the body.

Blood and digestion

Some blood travels along *arteries* to the small *intestine*. There, nutrients produced by the digestive system from the food we take in, such as sugars and *fats*, enter the blood. This blood flows along the portal *vein*, carrying nutrients to the liver. The liver turns them into chemicals the body needs or stores them for later use. The liver releases new chemicals back into the blood for transportation to the cells.

Waste transport

Cells release waste products from the processes that happen inside them. For example, in a *muscle* cell, oxygen and glucose combine to release energy. A waste product from this process is the *gas* carbon dioxide. Carbon dioxide is carried to the lungs, where it is breathed out. Some carbon dioxide is carried by the red blood cells, but most is carried dissolved in plasma. Other waste chemicals are carried to the liver to be turned into less harmful chemicals. The blood carries the less harmful chemicals to the kidneys to be expelled from the body in *urine*.

Hormones

Blood also carries *hormones* throughout the body. Hormones are part of the body's control system, called the endocrine system. They are made in the endocrine *glands* and released into the blood. Hormones work as chemical "messengers," controlling important functions of the body.

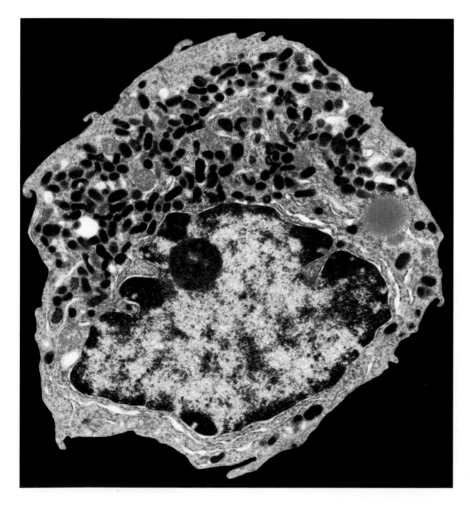

FAQ

Q. What is epinephrine?

A. Epinephrine, also spelled epinephrin, is a hormone released into the blood by the adrenal gland when a person is in a frightening or stressful situation. Epinephrine is also called adrenalin, sometimes spelled adrenaline. Epinephrine makes the heart rate and breathing speed up and opens up arteries to carry more blood to the muscles, helping the body respond more efficiently to stress.

This is an endocrine cell. Its job is to produce hormones that are transported throughout the body in the blood.

Fighting infection

Blood is an important part of the immune system, which fights infections in the body. Infections are caused by such foreign bodies as *bacteria* and *viruses*. After getting into the body, these germs multiply and spread. White blood *cells* (see pages 22–23) are the body's main defense against these invaders. On their surfaces, all bacteria and viruses have a unique pattern of chemicals, known as antigens. The body's own cells have antigens, too. The disease fighters in your body use each cell's antigens to tell friend from enemy.

Inflammation

A micrograph of two T lymphocytes attached to a cancer cell. They have recognized a foreign antigen on the surface of the cell.

One of the body's first reactions to germs is to create an inflammation. The blood vessels in the area attacked by the germ widen, allowing more blood—and with it more disease fighters—to reach the site of the infection. This increased flow of blood causes redness, swelling, and sometimes pain in the affected part.

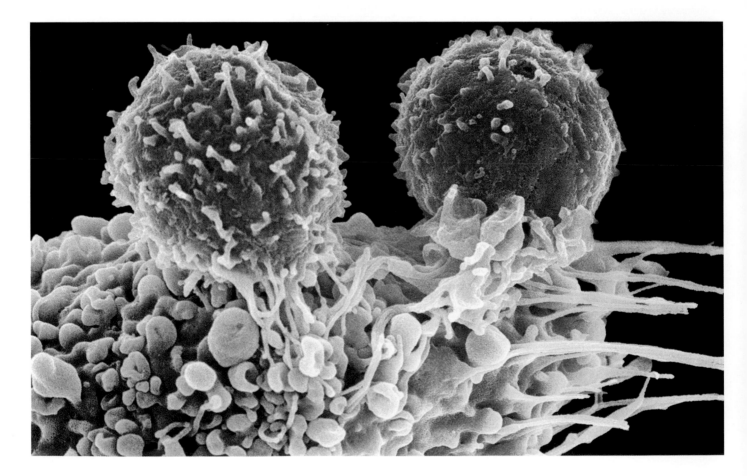

Engulfing germs

Some white blood cells fight germs by engulfing (swallowing) them and then digesting them. These cells are the phagocytes. The jellylike phagocytes wrap themselves around the germ and swallow it up.

Killer cells

Some white cells, called T lymphocytes, recognize antigens on germs. Each T cell recognizes a different antigen. The T cells attach themselves to the antigens and kill the germ. They also reproduce themselves quickly to kill off any more of the same germ.

Making antibodies

B lymphocytes fight in a different way. When they attach themselves to the antigen on a germ, they divide, making many new cells that produce chemicals called antibodies. The antibodies move through the blood, killing the germs where they find them.

Some of the B lymphocytes formed during an infection remember how to make the antibodies to kill the germ. These lymphocytes stay in the blood or lymph nodes (see pages 38–39) for up to 20 years or more, waiting to release antibodies to kill off the germ quickly if it returns. The body is therefore said to be immune to that germ.

A vaccination introduces a mild form of a virus or bacteria into the body. This makes the body immune to more serious forms of the disease.

FAQ

Q. **What is AIDS?**

A. **AIDS stands for "acquired immunodeficiency syndrome." It is a serious disease that keeps the immune system from working properly. AIDS is caused by a virus called the human immunodeficiency virus (HIV). As white blood cells try to fight the virus, the virus keeps them from working. This makes it hard for the person infected with HIV to fight other infections. HIV is transmitted (moves) from one person to another by contact of an uninfected person with such bodily fluids as the blood of an infected person.**

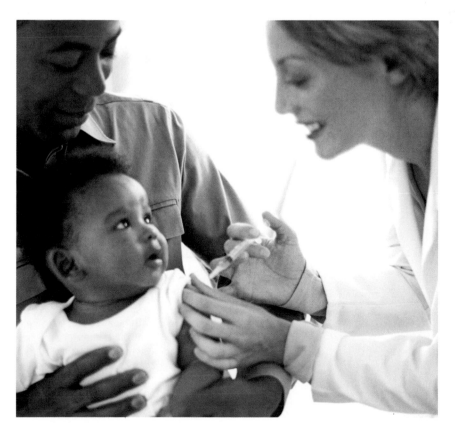

The lymphatic system

The circulatory system is not the only system of vessels in the body. The lymphatic system is similar to the network of vessels in the circulatory system, but it carries a different kind of liquid.

Liquid passes through the walls of the *capillaries*, carrying oxygen, *nutrients*, and other chemicals with it. The liquid flows into the space between *cells*, where it is called interstitial fluid. The interstitial fluid is collected by a network of vessels and returned to the blood. Once the fluid is inside the vessels, it is called lymph.

Lymphatic vessels

The lymphatic system collects lymph from all over body. It is a drainage system for lymph. The vessels are extremely small to start with, but they join to form larger vessels that carry more lymph. Inside the vessels are *valves* that keep the lymph from flowing the wrong way. All the lymph vessels lead to a tube called the thoracic duct in the base of the neck, where the lymph rejoins the circulatory system and becomes part of the blood again.

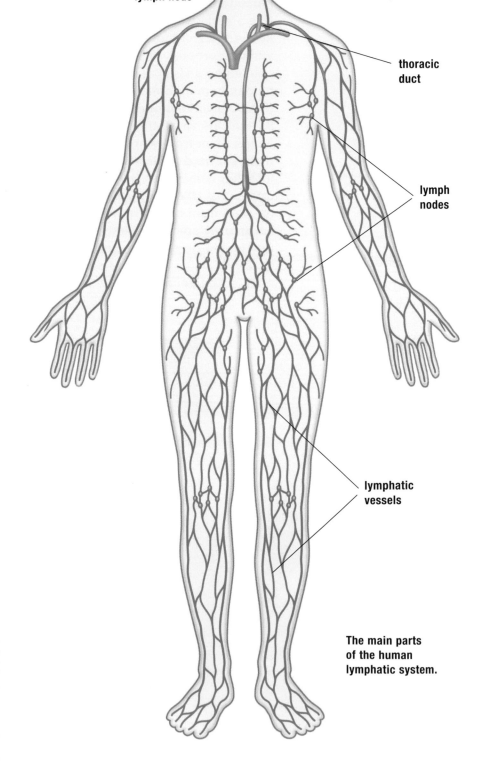

lymph node

thoracic duct

lymph nodes

lymphatic vessels

The main parts of the human lymphatic system.

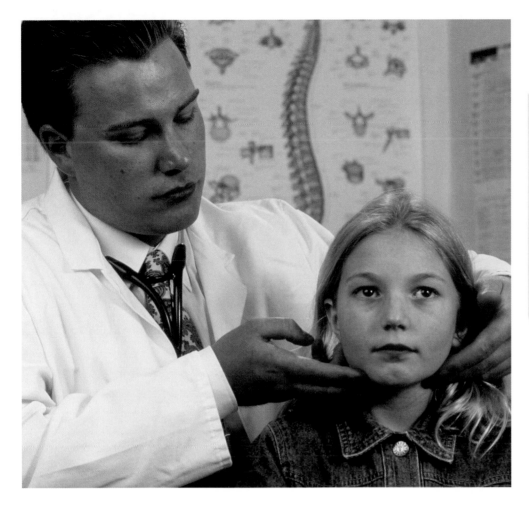

FAQ

Q. What are swollen glands?

A. Swollen glands are not really glands, but swollen and sore lymph nodes. They are a sign of infection. Inside the lymph nodes, millions of white cells being produced to fight the infection cause the swelling.

Swelling at the top and front of the neck is caused by enlarged lymph nodes. It is a sign that the body is fighting infection.

Lymph nodes

In many places in the body the lymph vessels widen out to form small lumps called lymph nodes. More lymph nodes are in some places than others. They are found especially in the neck, under the arms, and above the groin, the area where the thighs join the abdomen. Lymph nodes are important in fighting disease. They are full of lymphocytes, which produce antibodies (see page 37). Other white cells called macrophages absorb dead tissue and other foreign particles in the lymph nodes.

Spleen

The spleen is one of the largest parts of the lymphatic system. It is behind the stomach, is about the size of a fist, and is purple in color. Macrophages in the spleen destroy parasites and *bacteria* and remove worn-out blood cells and *platelets* from the blood that flows through the spleen.

Blood and blood vessel problems

Various diseases and disorders prevent the blood from circulating and working efficiently. In extreme cases the blood supply to an organ or other part of the body is cut off completely, and the cells there may die.

The misshapen red blood cells of a person suffering from sickle-cell anemia.

Lack of oxygen

Anemia is a disease in which the blood cannot transport enough oxygen. The main symptoms are breathlessness, tiredness, and pale skin. Anemia is caused when red blood cells do not carry oxygen properly or a person does not have enough red blood cells.

Sickle cell anemia is caused by red blood cells that are the wrong shape. These red blood cells are long and twisted. They can not carry as much oxygen as normal red blood cells. Sickle cell anemia principally afflicts African Americans in the United States. It also affects people of Central African, Mediterranean, Middle Eastern, and Indian heritage.

Blocking the arteries

Narrowed *arteries* cut down the amount of blood that can flow through the circulatory system. Arteries become narrower when fatty deposits called plaques form on their walls. This usually happens when a person eats too much fatty food. Eventually plaques can block an artery completely. Partly blocked arteries are a major cause of high blood pressure. High blood pressure can damage the heart and other organs of the body.

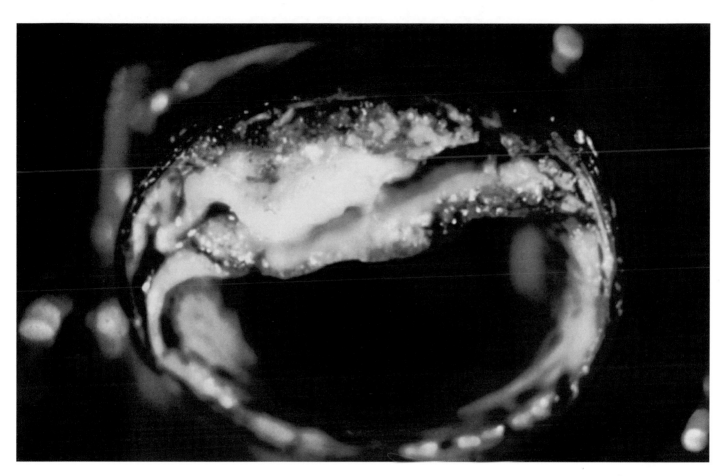

An end-on view of an artery that is clogged with fatty deposits.

As people age, their arteries lose their stretchiness and become harder. This prevents the artery walls from helping to push the blood along.

Blood clots

Blood can clot inside blood vessels when the smooth flow of blood is stopped, such as when an artery is partly blocked by plaques. If the clot breaks off the wall of the blood vessel, the clot is carried around in the blood until it reaches a blood vessel that is too narrow for it to pass through. This vessel becomes blocked, cutting off the blood supply. Blocking of an artery leading to the brain, the heart, or the *lungs* can be life threatening.

FAQ

Q. What is DVT?

A. DVT, or deep-vein thrombosis, is a blood clot that forms in a vein deep inside a leg. It can be caused by being inactive for many hours. Some long-distance airline passengers claim to have suffered from DVT. DVT causes leg pain and swelling. In the worst cases, the clot breaks away and becomes stuck in an artery to the lungs. The person then can not breathe properly. In these cases the person must go to a hospital where he or she is treated with drugs to dissolve the blood clot or have an operation to remove the clot.

Heart disease

Normally the heart beats for a whole lifetime without any problems. But sometimes the heart stops working properly. The most common cause of this is coronary artery disease, which cuts off the supply of oxygen to the heart *muscles*.

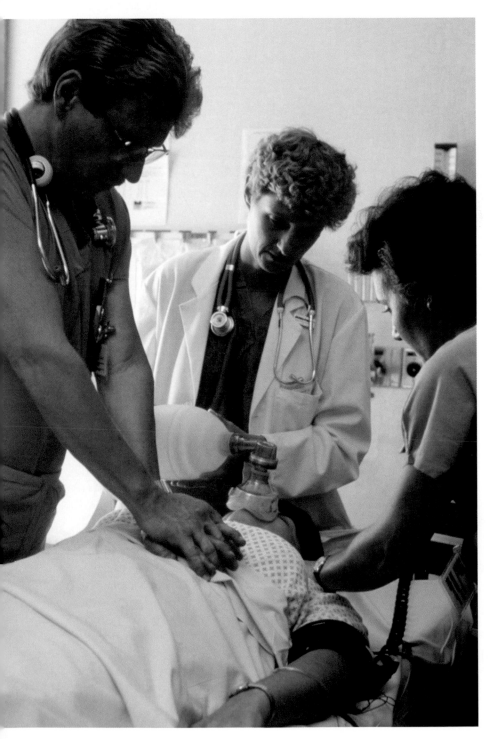

Some heart problems happen because the heart is not formed properly or because parts fail. For example, some children are born with a hole between the two atria or the two ventricles in the heart. Heart *valves* can fail, keeping the heart from pumping efficiently. These defects normally can be corrected by surgery.

Coronary problems

The *coronary arteries* carry blood to the heart muscles. If these arteries become narrowed or blocked, the heart muscles are starved of oxygen and the heart stops beating properly. The blockage can be caused by coronary artery disease or by a blood clot from elsewhere in the body.

Angina is pain in the chest caused by an insufficient supply of oxygen to the heart muscles. The pain is normally felt during exercise or at times of stress, when the heart needs more oxygen than usual.

A patient in cardiac arrest (the heart has stopped beating) being given a heart massage to keep the blood flowing.

A heart attack is caused by the sudden loss of the blood supply to a part of the cardiac muscle. This loss damages the muscle within minutes. A heart attack can cause the heart to fibrillate, or beat rapidly without pumping blood, or to stop completely, which is called cardiac arrest.

Heart treatments

Coronary artery disease can be relieved by drugs, but sometimes the only answer is surgery. One technique is called angioplasty, in which a small balloon is put into the coronary artery to try to widen it. Heart bypass surgery is more complicated. The blocked coronary artery is bypassed, or avoided, with a section of *vein* taken from somewhere else in the body. For some patients a heart transplant is needed. The whole heart is removed and replaced by a heart from a donor.

FAQ

Q. Can someone get an artificial heart?

A. Several artificial hearts have been built. Each artificial heart includes a mechanical pump to move the blood, and valves to make sure the blood flows the right way. Artificial hearts are still not common, and much research is needed before anyone can make an artificial heart that is as reliable as the real thing.

A surgeon placing a Jarvik-7 artificial heart into a patient's chest cavity. The Jarvik-7 heart was developed in the 1980's.

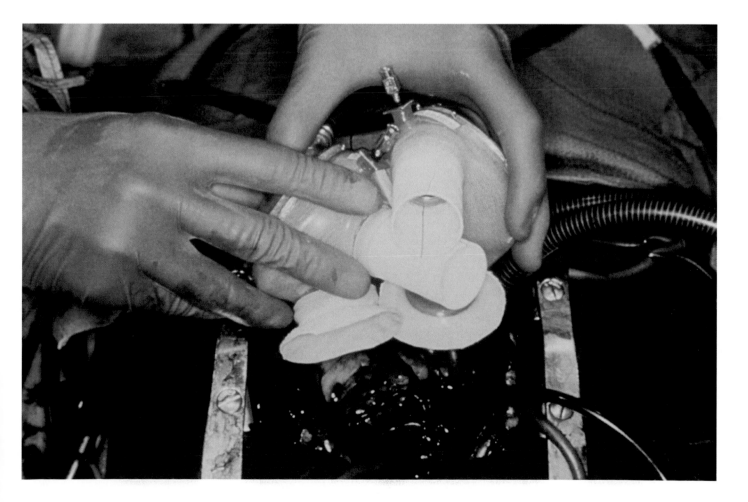

Healthy circulation

Today, medicines and surgery can help people with diseases of the heart and the blood vessels (known as cardiovascular diseases). However, in developed countries, heart disease is the leading cause of death because many people in those countries eat fatty foods and do not get enough exercise.

Most people who suffer from cardiovascular disease are middle-aged or elderly. But the best time to think about keeping your circulatory system healthy is when you are young. Looking after your heart and blood vessels now will help them last a lifetime.

So what is the secret to having a healthy circulatory system? The answer is simple. You should eat a balanced diet, exercise regularly, and not smoke cigarettes.

Green leafy vegetables, such as those shown in the photograph, are rich in iron, needed to make new red blood cells. Clockwise from top: green curly kale, cabbage, and chard.

FAQs

Q. Does stress cause heart attacks?

A. Stress caused by such things as a difficult job or home life does not cause a heart attack on its own. But stress is dangerous for a person who already has cardiovascular disease. Stress increases the heart rate and blood pressure, which can trigger a heart attack.

A balanced diet

To avoid circulation problems, eating a balanced diet, containing a good mixture of the different food types, is important. The different food types are *carbohydrates*, *fats*, *proteins*, *vitamins*, and *minerals*.

The main cause of cardiovascular disease is eating too much fatty food. The body needs fats to work properly, but too much fat—especially a fat called cholesterol—leads to blocked *arteries*.

Your diet should not include too much salt, which is one cause of high blood pressure. The mineral iron is needed for healthy blood, because the *hemoglobin* in blood contains iron. Good sources of iron are red meat, whole grains, and green vegetables.

Exercise

Regular exercise, such as walking, running, cycling, and swimming, helps to keep the heart healthy. Such activities exercise the cardiac *muscles*, making the heart more efficient at pumping. Exercise also helps the arteries to stay stretchy. Exercise uses up energy, which helps to keep people from becoming overweight, a cause of high blood pressure.

Smoking

The chemicals in inhaled cigarette smoke enter the blood and encourage the buildup of plaques in the arteries. Nicotine from tobacco makes the heart pump faster, which can overwork it. So not smoking cigarettes and staying away from places where people are smoking are ways to reduce the chances of getting cardiovascular disease.

Regular exercise helps to keep the circulatory system in good working order.

Glossary

aorta The major blood vessel through which blood travels away from the heart to the body.

artery A thick-walled blood vessel through which blood travels away from the heart to the body or lungs.

bacteria Microorganisms made up of a single cell.

capillary An extremely narrow blood vessel from which substances pass from the blood into the body tissues and from the tissues into the blood.

carbohydrate One of the main types of nutrient in food that the digestive system breaks down for energy.

cell The basic building block of the body. The body contains hundreds of different types of cells, such as blood cells, skin cells, and nerve cells.

coronary artery An artery through which blood travels to the heart's muscles.

fat One of the main types of nutrient in food that the digestive system breaks down for energy.

formed elements The cells and pieces of cells in the blood: red cells, white cells, and platelets.

gas One of the three states of matter, the others being solid and liquid. Oxygen is a gas.

gland A part of the body that makes special chemicals for the body.

glucose A type of sugar that the body uses as a source of energy.

hemoglobin The chemical in red blood cells that carries oxygen.

hormone A chemical that controls how some parts of the body work.

intestines The small and large intestines are part of the digestive system. Substances from digested food pass from the intestines into the blood.

lungs The two lungs are the major organs of the respiratory system. Oxygen passes from the lungs into the blood. Carbon dioxide passes from the blood into the lungs.

minerals Simple chemicals, such as iron and sodium, that the body needs in small amounts.

molecule A tiny particle that makes up many materials. Molecules are made up of atoms joined together.

muscle A type of body tissue that can contract under the control of nerves.

nerve A long, thin bundle of cells that carries electric signals throughout the body to control muscles, organs, and other body parts.

nucleus (plural: nuclei) The central part of a living cell.

nutrient A substance in food that your body needs to work properly.

plasma The liquid part of the blood, left after the formed elements are removed from it.

platelet One of the formed elements in the blood. Platelets play a part in blood clotting.

protein A type of nutrient in food that the digestive system breaks down to allow the body to grow and repair itself.

stethoscope A device used to listen to sounds in a person's chest.

tissue A part of the body made from cells that are all similar. Muscles are one kind of tissue, and skin is another.

urine A mixture of water and waste products that is made in the kidneys and passed out of the body.

valve A device that controls the flow of liquid. One-way valves in the circulatory system prevent blood from flowing in the wrong direction.

vein A thin-walled blood vessel through which blood travels from the body and lungs back to the heart.

virus A very tiny particle that can infect the cells of living things and cause disease.

vitamin A chemical that is needed to make certain body processes work properly.

Additional resources

Books

Ballard, Carol. *Exploring the Human Body: The Heart and Circulation.* San Diego, CA: KidHaven Press, 2005.

Mehler, Robert E. *How the Circulatory System Works.* Malden, MA: Blackwell Science, 2001.

Whitfield, Philip, ed. *The Human Body Explained: A Guide to Understanding the Incredible Living Machine.* New York: Henry Holt, 1995.

Web sites

http://kidshealth.org/kid/body/heart_noSW.html
An entertaining guide to the heart and other body parts.

http://www.idahoptv.org/dialogue4kids/season4/blood/facts.html
A look at blood—what it is, what it is for, and what it is made of.

http://www.fi.edu/biosci/heart.html
An exploration of the human heart.

Index